Confessions of a Principal

30 Proven Principles TO <u>LEAD BY</u>

Confessions of a Principal

30 Proven Principles TO <u>LEAD BY</u>

Patrick S. Muhammad, ED.S

PSM Enterprises & Services, LLC

Other Books by
Patrick S. Muhammad

Little Librarian Girl

Wear My Shoes, Please!

Mom, Where's My Dad?

The Principal Farmer

Copyright © 2012 by Patrick S. Muhammad

All rights reserved. No part of this publication may be reproduced, distributed, or transmitted in any form or by any means, including photocopying, recording, or other electronic or mechanical methods, without the prior written permission requests, write to publisher, addressed "Attention Permissions Coordinator" at the address below.

PSM Enterprises & Services
c/o RATHSI Publishing, LLC.
Tel: (404) 207-0544
www.rathsipublishingllc.com

ORDERING INFORMATION
Quantity sales. Special discounts are available on quantity purchases by corporations, associations, and other. For details, contact the "Special Sales Department" at the RATHSI Publishing address above.

RATHSI Publishing and the RATHSI Publishing logo are registered trademarks of PSM Enterprises. www.psmenterprises.com

Printed in the United States of America

Library of Congress 2012906409
ISBN 978-1-936937-52-3 Paperback

"Remember, the only way to achieve success is to Reach Back and take someone with you." - PSM

Dedicated to those who wake everyday to raise and shape the future of this world, educators are born, not trained. -PSM

"Be You, who God desired in his mind for you to be. Do You, what God has whispered in your ear to do. Don't Change for Nobody, He made you the way you are. Don't Change for no Amount, it will never be enough to go against God's plan for you!" -PSM

"Planting Seeds In Minds To Grow America!"- PSM

Confessions of a PRINCIPAL

Why This Book?
Introduction

Confessions

1. Don't fake the best, be the best.
2. One person's trash, another person's treasure.
3. No second chance to make a first judgement
4. Three-Month Budget
5. If the intent is meant for good, take the risk.
6. Say What you mean and Mean what you SEE
7. Starbucks draws a crowd
8. Let situations bring about conversations
9. Don't Get Bullied
10. Culture of Collaborative Communication
11. If you pass it, they will too.
12. There is Power in NO
13. Answer the phone.
14. Boomerang, I wanna know everything
15. The buck stops here.
16. @the fork in the road, Trailblazers go straight.
17. Surround yourself with Einstein's
18. You are not a hero until you save something or someone
19. Used to Be's don't make any honey
20. Systems outlive people
21. Volleying with your adversaries
22. Bon Voyage to Your Island
23. Postmaster Stamps it All

24. The choir harmonizes, the individual sings a solo.
25. Imma, Imma, Do it first, then talk about.
26. I Apologize
27. Finding a mentor
28. If it doesn't exist, make it.
29. Run Through The Tape
30. Courageous Conversations

Recommended Book List

About the Author

WHY THIS BOOK?

The book is a summary of what to expect throughout your school years as the Principal. As you sit behind your clean desk and begin to make those critical decisions, you will soon find out that you have a handicap. That handicap is the lights are off on your leadership. This initially may serve as an impediment to your leadership. However, when used properly you can be effective, even in the dark.

The reason you are in the dark is do to the fact that you do not know what to expect and cannot see what is ahead of you. You want to plan the school's schedule, teacher assignments, building adjustments, budgeting responsibilities and many other envisioned task, but you do not know what you do not know.

The only way to see in the dark is to be still, be quiet, relax, and let the light come to you. When you begin to let this be your daily routine, your eyes will adjust to the dark. In the dark, you will be able to see the shape and/ or outline of objects, but the details of that object will remain difficult to make out. You are going to bump into objects, scrap your leg on the edge of obstacles, trip over items, and even fall down. This journey through the dark will sometimes seem impossible, but it is necessary. Just as you have to navigate through darkness, so will your staff, parents, students, and community. You have to stay the course and make it through to the light.

Can you see in the dark? Keep reading this book, take notes, remember the Confessions, and turn the light on your leadership.

INTRODUCTION

Ahhhhhhhhhhh. Finally, that sigh of relief that we all anticipated having one day. After the many years of anticipation, hesitation, procrastination, dedication, and exhaustion, the day has finally come. You are leaving the ranks of being the second in charge, the 'little' cheese, the other administrator, or whatever nickname you were referred as. You are now the Principal.

For many, this job has eluded you for many years. You have applied, interviewed, and been denied that perfect promotion, at the ideal school, time and time again. You have rode by and superstitiously parked in the Principal parking spot of several schools, hoping this would be the one. You've worn that lucky suit unluckily over 10 times. Prepared the most detailed and scripted answers for potential interview questions and memorized your follow up responses. However, after all that preparation, for some reason outside of your control, the powers that "Be" selected someone else.

But now, the fact that you are holding this book in your hands means this is your day, your time, and your season. Or you are speaking your future by studying the Confessions that follow.

I to shared these same feelings for nine and a half years. I was on the fast track out of the classroom and into administration and was forecast to become Principal in no time. However, nobody put a time frame on "no time". I sat through over 8 interviews for position all over. I even sat through board meetings waiting to hear my name announced as the new Principal. But for some reason, the powers that be had other plans.

Finally, my day arrived. I was so excited that I was numb for the first few weeks. All those years of saying what I would do if I was... Those meetings as assistant principal we sat through and inside said, "I can't believe this is the direction we are going!" My time had finally come.

What happened next only enhanced the numbing affect. I went in to sign my contract and noticed that I had under calculated the raise some (OK, I could live with that). I received the keys to the building, the alarm code, and a firm "congratulations." I was still waiting for that last secret to the Principalship, you know the step-by-step guide to running my building. I was waiting on the instructions on making gains, benchmarks, increasing staff morale, handling irate parents, and balancing the schools budget. The only caveat was all of this happened in my car in front of the county office, SOLO.

Let me be the first to tell you, there is no guide or secret meeting to running your school as Principal. In administration you will learn that everybody else's moment is more important than your moment, and there is no time set aside to help the principals. On the job training is just that, on the job in between the chaos of running the building.

Remember, it's your day, your time, your season, and YOUR Responsibility. Take this book to heart, because it was written from the heart. This book is for those who come behind me, you will not have to start from scratch.

Confession :

1. An open declaration of something about one's self.

2. To give evidence of.

3. **A statement of one's principles.**

"WE ARE WHAT WE REPEATEDLY DO. EXCELLENCE, THEN, IS NOT AN ACT, BUT A HABIT."
-ARISTOTLE

DON'T FAKE THE BEST, BE THE BEST.

CONFESSION- 1

There was a saying I would often hear growing up, "fake it till you make it." I never knew the origin of this saying, however, I found myself using it from time to time. One day in a casual conversation with a seasoned educator, she scorned me for using the saying. She emphatically reprimanded me for using such a saying in any form or context as it related to myself. She then went on to remind me of my many accomplishments and achievements throughout the years she'd known me.

This brief interaction leads us into our first confession, "Don't fake the best, be the best!" **Confession- 1**

As leader of your building, it is necessary that you demonstrate the highest level of know how and the deepest level of humility. The know how you will demonstrate through task, obstacles, situations, and as problems present themselves. The humility must arise when you do not have the expertise in situations. It is at that point you exercise humility and acknowledge what you do not know. Always remember, " the biggest room in the house, is the room for improvement." When you acknowledge what you do not know, you allow yourself to fill that void with new information, thus eliminating areas of personal deficiencies.

Additionally, you show your staff that it is OK for them not to know everything, because you have shown your vunerablility that you don't know everyting. In this ever evolving/ digital universe, new information emerges every millisecond of the day. When you admit your areas of improvement, it will aid your staff in identifying theirs and place them on a journey to improvement.

The opposite of humility is overt arrogance. Taking on a posture of "Know it all" closes the energies of growth amongst any organization. When the Principal has this thwarted demeanor, an intended place of learning becomes a valley of isolated pockets filled with disconnected members, afraid to venture out into the world of, "I don't know."

Not knowing is the greatest experience to educational conquest. "A man in search of water will not stop until his thirst is quenched. Likewise, a man who goes out in search of knowledge shall never return." When you erroneously believe you "Know It all", you stop growing and stop searching for new knowledge. This destroys your leadership and attracting influence to potential followers. What right-minded staff will follow a decaying leader. But a leader who is constantly training and conditioning their mind for an adventurous educational diaspora is one who is not faking the best, but becoming the best.

**DON'T FAKE THE BEST,
BE THE BEST.**

CONFESSION- 1

ELLWOOD CUBBERLEY SAID IN 1919......

"AS GOES THE PRINCIPAL SO GOES THE SCHOOL..."

ONE PERSON'S TRASH, ANOTHER PERSON'S TREASURE.

CONFESSION- 2

Do you remember hearing the theme song from the TV sitcom, Sanford and Son? As the theme music played, the camera panned the property of Fred Sanford. In your opinion, all you saw was trash and insignificance. To Fred, he would not have traded for the world what he had on that property. What Fred understood was, "One person's trash is another person's treasure." **CONFESSION- 2**

As a new principal in a building you are unfamiliar with, nothing is trash yet. I know you have the desire to beautify your new office and give it your personal flare. However, you don't know what gems are hidden and buried in your predecessor's piles of "trash."

I remember searching for a Title I document that was past due. I was not sure if I previously sent the document, drafted the document, or had not begun to formulate the information needed. After missing the deadline and making that dreaded phone call to the Title I department, I was relieved to hear on the other end, that the material I was desperately searching for was part of a previous years proposal and only my signature was needed on the old document. This is a small example of the treasures that are buried in your new office. Remember, success or failure, your predecessor had experience, events, agendas, letters, referrals, recommendations, grants, business partners, and more that are now at your disposal. This information can assist you in formulating and outlining reports, instead of pulling from thin air and relying on your creativity.

Additionally, you don't want to throw out the baby with the bath water.

Often times, there is not a smooth transition of the principalship due to the complexities that arise when vacancies exist. There is rarely an opportunity to sit with the former principal, discuss staff, budgets, goals, etc. With this in mind, don't go into a new building and clean house. Meaning, you don't know what staff members will become beneficial to your administrative goals.

The strategies I have used include surveys (individual/ electronic*)and staff goal forms. The most effective tool I have used is informal/formal individual meetings with staff. This is where they will tell you everything you need to know (and a little of what you don't want to know). Though this can become time consuming, it allows you the opportunity to hear directly from your current staff. From these conversations, you can formulate your own opinions regarding the staff of the building.

Sometimes, the information you receive from previous administration can be tainted and the administrator might have a part to play in the staff members low performance. Not getting a feel for the staff yourself, you may in haste get rid of someone else's trash that could end up being a treasure for you.

"THE QUICKEST WAY TO CHANGE THE EFFECTIVENESS OF A SCHOOL (FOR BETTER OR WORSE) IS TO CHANGE THE PRINCIPAL."

−JAMES H. STRONGE

NO SECOND CHANCE TO MAKE A FIRST JUDGEMENT

CONFESSION- 3

Have you ever approached a person from the rear, believing you know the person from their silhouette? When the person turns around and its not who you believed it to be. The disappointment from it not being who you thought it was can set you back a moment.

Now let's change the dynamics of the person you are approaching. As you are approaching the person, you begin to berate the person for reasons unknowing to you or to the person. You have formulated in your mind that this person is in violation of a rule you live by. As the person turns around, again, it's not the person you believed it was, and they are not guilty of what you berated them initially for. This time, the results are detrimental. You have placed judgement upon this person, and now you have to retreat.

When this occurs, you will never be able to turn back the hands of time and get a second chance to make a first judgement.

Confession- 3

That judgement in error places barriers and roadblocks in the relationship with this person. What if the person is a parent, student, teacher, community stakeholder, or colleague? It doesn't matter who the person is, but it matters how the situation is handled.

As a Principal, you have to always err on the side of caution. NEVER MAKE A DECISION, COMMENT, FINDING, OR DETERMINATION without first getting ALL

THE FACTS. You may have a track record of making good judgements when placed in situations needing quick results, but never make a decision, comment, finding, or determination again without getting all the facts. I know I repeated that same sentence twice and that's how important it is.

When you give a decision, its final (or so you believe). Students, Parents, & Staff have rights and due process. When you give a decree, you want it to be final, but if you in haste make a decision without all the facts, you open yourself up to erring on the side of making a decision and not making the right decision.

An example of this occurred in taking over a building. I was reviewing test scores and noticed a teacher had some horrific results, really deplorable. I relied on the previous administration placement of that teacher in a lower grade, because that teacher was obviously ineffective in the previous grade.(**Remember Confession- 2**)

As the year progressed, I noticed the parents were consistently requesting conferences with this teacher. Based on the previous administrator's decision, I just knew these were conferences that were engaged with disgust of having such an inadequate educator in charge of their student's educational career.

Finally, I stopped a parent and asked if they didn't mind sharing the nature of the conference. To my surprise, the parent shared that the teacher was taking time to meet with each individual parent to have " Courageous Conversations" about their children's academic levels and goals. The frequency of these conferences was due to the number of students in the class (27 and growing). Additionally, parents had to sign a class contract to assist with the goals set by the teacher. What the previous administration failed to share was the previous school year, this misjudged teacher had 16 EIP students (below grade level) that were at least two grade levels below their grade level counterparts. After one year with this "inadequate" teacher, the students improved. Even though compared to their grade level counterparts they scored lower, these 16 students were able to close their deficient levels by a grade level in one years time. (Statistically Amazing).

Take time in formulating your opinions and actions, you never get a second chance to make a first judgement.

NO SECOND CHANCE TO MAKE A FIRST JUDGEMENT

CONFESSION- 3

"THE ROLE OF THE LEADER IS TO ENSURE THAT THE ORGANIZATION DEVELOPS RELATIONSHIPS THAT HELP PRODUCE DESIRABLE RESULTS."
—M. FULLAN

THREE-MONTH BUDGET

CONFESSION- 4

The financial practices of a Principal are make or break, there is no in between. While many pre- certification programs may offer a class or two on financial fidelity, it's nothing like the day-to-day financial decisions you will be obligated to oversee.

One of the most glaring realities for me during the first year of Principalship was that the large budget sheet you received at the beginning of the school term quickly dwindles in a short period of time. Unlike your monthly paycheck, this budget is it for the entire year. If you spend your budget in the first couple of months, you will be out of funds for the rest of the year. To avoid this from occurring, I have devised what I call the Three- Month Budget. **CONFESSION-4**

My bookkeeper has divided my budget allotment into four three-month budgets. For Example, if your budget is 100K. Every three months, you only have 25K to spend, that's it. Now that sounds simple, but its a little more complex. The complexity comes in the fact, that most budgets have to be exhausted in a short period of time.

Title I budgets have to be set aside before the funds arrive. You will have to spend the preliminary funds in a template and once the funds are released on the district level, your items in the template will then be purchased. This is the physical spending of the budget, however our confession requires the planning in a three- month budget cycle.

Take your time and assess what are your needs for your school. Don't get in the terrible principal habit of just buying things to get off the list of principals not having turned their budgets in by the "time line." This will fill your building with "stuff" that will never be used by the students or teachers and will not improve the overall success of your building.

Spend the money on the needs of your building that will benefit the students. Do you need to improve your mathematics department? Which grade levels need the most support; which teachers need staff development and when is the training for that development occurring; what manipulatives are needed to improve your mathematical deficiencies? Once you answer these or similar questions, your budget is based on these priorities.

The key is to only handle what can be accomplished in three months. Even though you may determine there are 20 "hot" items on your needs list for improvement. Only handle the hottest, a few at a time.

Have you ever heard the adage, "don't bite off more than you can chew?" You can't heal all the ills of your school at one time, however, if you prioritize and have a plan on which areas to tackle at a time, you will begin to make effective progress.

A little nugget of wisdom, when you take this approach, you may arrive at the third 3-month cycle and realize your list of 20 is down to 8. Why? Some areas are by-products of larger problems. When you address the large problems you eliminate the smaller by-products of the larger problem.

Take the time to implement this confession. The time you put in to ensure the allotted funds are spent to address needs will payoff in the long run and address your your students needs.

THREE-MONTH BUDGET

CONFESSION- 4

"IT IS ONLY WITH THE HEART THAT ONE CAN SEE RIGHTLY; WHAT IS ESSENTIAL IS INVISIBLE TO THE EYE."
- ANTOINE DE SAINT-EXUPERY

IF THE INTENT IS MEANT FOR GOOD, TAKE THE RISK.

CONFESSION- 5

As an avid reader of educational practices, I came across countless studies in which single- gender settings propelled academic achievement. While the research proved this true, many school systems, schools, and Principals were reluctant to take the calculated risk. Throughout your career as a Principal, some risks have to be taken, if the intent is meant for good. **CONFESSION- 5**

I decided to take the risk as it related to single-gender classes. My supervisor told me that this could mean continued tenure as a Principal or open the opportunity for a quick demotion.

I reviewed the research, set my team in place and implemented single gender in 5th grade. One Girl's Class, One Boy's Class, and One Mixed Gender Class. I consulted the teachers and only asked them to do their best.

At the conclusion of the school year, the all girls class scored 100% proficiency in Reading, English Language Arts, and 92% in Mathematics. The all boys class, 96% Reading, English Language Arts, and 88% in Mathematics. Both groups out scored the mixed group by over 15%.

Remember, at this point in your career, nobody wants to be wrong and/ or to blame. You will have supervisors who can guide you, but remember they have to protect their jobs as well. So when you have the gut feeling, and your intent is of good, go ahead and take the risk.

" TO BE PERSUASIVE WE MUST BE BELIEVABLE; TO BE BELIEVABLE WE MUST BE CREDIBLE; TO BE CREDIBLE WE MUST BE TRUTHFUL."
– EDWARD R. MURROW

SAY WHAT YOU MEAN AND MEAN WHAT YOU SEE

CONFESSION- 6

The most effective leaders of all time have vision unlike those that follow them. Thus, that's what makes them the leader. Your vision is quality, characteristic, and gift that others may not have. Your vision will often, if not always, cause your ideas to seem strange, far fetched, and to your staff, impossible. In order to make progress towards your vision you have to say what you mean and mean what you see.

CONFESSION- 6

During the first month of school, I shared with my leadership staff that I wanted to have a State of the School Address and get all 500 (School population 497) families in our building to attend. The look on my leadership staff's faces was like "sticker shock" when signing home mortgage papers and seeing how much interest you will pay in 30 years. My team, though doubtful, didn't want to show immediate dissension from the plan.

Within thirty days, we created a buzz around the school. We involved every grade level, department, and community liaisons in the program.

We invited Board members, the media, and surrounding principals.

Not only did we surpass our goal of 500 in attendance, we had over 700 in attendance who stayed the entire 2-hour program (***how was it done? Call me).

All stakeholders have to know that your word is better than gold. When you take a stand, stakeholders once confident in you, will rely on you. This level of commitment is a two way street. The stakeholders will remain committed to you as long as your word remains as dependable as you allow it to be.

Say what you mean, even in difficult times, mean what you say, even when it may not be in your favor and you will have support from stakeholders unmatched.

SAY WHAT YOU MEAN AND MEAN WHAT YOU SEE

CONFESSION- 6

"NEVER ABORT YOUR VISION DUE TO THE LACK OF AGREEMENT BY THE MASSES. NO BUILDING HAS EIGHT PRINCIPALS OR EVEN TWO PRINCIPALS. YOU ARE THE ONE CHOSEN TO LEAD. LEAD, IF YOU DON'T, YOU WILL BE LED."
−PSM

STARBUCKS DRAWS A CROWD

CONFESSION- 7

It amazes me when I visit the local coffee shops. The crowds gather over coffee and a conversation. Many bring their laptops, chess games, newspaper, magazine, etc. The most intriguing part of visiting a coffee shop is the conversations. The ability to dialogue, discuss, and debate the latest scoop, gossip, theory, with strangers or better stated, people who can't change the realities of the topics being discussed. Something about the Starbucks Coffee, it draws a crowd.

Confession- 7

This also happens in schools everyday. That one coffee pot in the teacher's lounge, can become the stirring pot of your schools daily dialogues, discussions, debates, and gossip. Some staff members make it their business to gather all the news for the day and begin to spread the morning report hot off the press around the coffee pot. Some information they may be privy to and the information might be true. Other information they just can't contain within themselves they just have to let it out.

I suggest two ways to handle the distracting information. The first way is to ignore whatever information is gathered, disseminated or divulged. This could work, but remember, " cancer spreads if not nipped in the bud!"

The second way is get yourself a cup of coffee even if your not a coffee drinker. This totally disrupts the flow of nonsense spread at the stirring pot. You won't have to get coffee everyday, but the fact that you will enter this space will prompt the frequenters to quickly get their serving and then get on to "on task" agendas.

One thing you will learn quickly, your presence at certain "hot spots" in your building will either be welcomed or unwanted. This simple building routine will encourage your staff to stay on task. Additionally, you want to create a culture of focusing on agenda items within your control. Situations that arise outside of your building and above your pay grade are not focal points of your's or your schools agenda. Either way, its in your favor to always be unpredictable. Cream or Sugar anyone? (Principal Smirk)

STARBUCKS DRAWS A CROWD

CONFESSION- 7

"LISTEN A LOT, SPEAK A LITTLE. ONE WORD IS ENOUGH TO MAKE A LOT OF TROUBLE. A FOOL SPEAKS A LOT, A WISE MAN THINKS INSTEAD. ONE WORD IS AS GOOD AS NINE."
-FINNISH PROVERB

LET SITUATIONS BRING ABOUT CONVERSATIONS

CONFESSION- 8

As a new leader, you are not going to be able to immediately put your hand on the pulse of everything happening in your building, initially. Some situations, you will have no idea of until you are right in the middle of solving them. Some situations you will not ever get a handle on and that's find. However, *let situations bring about conversations*. **CONFESSIONS- 8**

Conversation must begin between those key stakeholders in your building. Don't assume ANYTHING. If you don't give the directive, follow-up on the agenda, or arrive early for the meeting, you cannot assume anything will get done.

When staff members come to you with problems, set the tone in the building that they must bring possible solutions. In their submitting problems to you, look carefully for the root of the problem. Often times, "the one bringing the bone is taking the bone!"

Problem starters by nature like to be acknowledged for making you aware of what's going on. Example, a district PTA representative arrived at a executive meeting one day and shared a random statement. In the statement, the representative shared that they received many complaints about a prior meetings procedures. The role they were taking was why and how was the meeting conducted and obviously some of my PTA were incompetent to the procedures to running the meeting, thus why they received so many complaints.

I then challenged the representative on the many complaints and inquired on an actual number. After further prodding, the many changed to few, then to two. Which in my mind was honestly none.

What you will soon realize, in being new and your first go around as the Boss, some people will try you. This trying of your leadership does not mean they won't support you, you have to establish 'Your Way' and mark your territory. Authority is not bestowed because you have the most keys now, sometimes, you will have to show your authority. Remember, you are the Judge and the Juror, court is never out of sessions until you say so.

LET SITUATIONS BRING ABOUT CONVERSATIONS

CONFESSION- 8

"THE CHALLENGE OF LEADERSHIP IS TO BE STRONG, BUT NOT RUDE; BE KIND, BUT NOT WEAK; BE BOLD, BUT NOT BULLY; BE THOUGHTFUL, BUT NOT LAZY; BE HUMBLE, BUT NOT TIMID; BE PROUD, BUT NOT ARROGANT; HAVE HUMOR, BUT WITHOUT FOLLY."
– JIM ROHN

DON'T GET BULLIED

CONFESSION - 9

Today, the word "bully" is the latest buzzword for parents, students, news agencies, and political figures. There have always been bullies and those being bullied since the first one room schoolhouse opened their doors to school age children. What's different today is the speed and spread of the apparent threat from bullies. Before, we had to wait for recess and then for the bully and bullied to be in the same place at the same time. Now, the bully or bullied can text, email, Facebook, or instant message the threat and the same method can be used to spread the rumour to hundreds or thousands instantly.

As Principal, there are two forms of bullying you have to get a hold of quick or you will get bullied. One fool proof way to handle this is, "don't get bullied."

Confession- 9

This is done on the student level and the staff level. There is a bully (student) that can't wait to get to the new Principal and there is a bully (staff member) that can't wait for your arrival. You have to have a plan to handle the bullies when they arrive.

With the student and staff, you have to win over the bully immediately. Notice I didn't say, "kiss up." ALL bullies bully because they have a need that has never been met. This need is your ticket to winning them over. On the student level, you want to find out what is their fear that causes them to act other than themselves.

The bullying aspect they use is a smoke screen to something they are hiding. Your task is to find out what it is.

The staff member is the same. There is a human need to be validated. Meaning to be acknowledged for the value you bring to whatever endeavour you pursue. The bully staff member often starves for this validation. It's your task to find out what that accomplishment is that hasn't been validated. Find it and you will have the bully on your side.

Now some veterans will say, don't waste your time with the bully, I disagree. All modern medicine teaches that cancer spreads unless it is treated in its early stages. This bully allowed to run loose in your building will infect the entire staff with their disdain for your administration. When this cancer takes over the entire school, you will be the one that's removed and the cancer will continue to find a host in the next Principal will become the victim. Don't get bullied.

DON'T GET BULLIED

CONFESSION- 9

> "TO LEAD PEOPLE, WALK BESIDE THEM ... AS FOR THE BEST LEADERS, THE PEOPLE DO NOT NOTICE THEIR EXISTENCE. THE NEXT BEST, THE PEOPLE HONOR AND PRAISE. THE NEXT, THE PEOPLE FEAR; AND THE NEXT, THE PEOPLE HATE ... WHEN THE BEST LEADER'S WORK IS DONE THE PEOPLE SAY, 'WE DID IT OURSELVES!'"
> – LAO-TZU

CULTURE OF COLLABORATIVE COMMUNICATION

CONFESSION- 10

The definition of communication requires that information is sent and received. Often times our communication is one directional. We send, but we don't ensure, that information is received and received in the manner in which we intended. In a culture of collaborative communication- **CONFESSION 10**, you focus on information not only disseminating from your office, but also coming from your stakeholders.

Many schools rest on the adage, we sent a flyer to the parents, and none of "them" showed up to conference night, PTA, etc.. However, these schools of thought never reach out to those they believe they are communicating with to see if the method used is effective or beneficial.

In a culture of collaborative communication, information flows on a continuous stream and may originate from outside of the intended flow. A Principal has to be open to receiving information from many sources. Even though stakeholders may only share information from their point of view, your role is to synthesize that information for the betterment of all stakeholders. If you cut off one aspect of communication, you will create pockets of misinformation and limit your affect or progress.

Since my assistant principal days, I have always stuck to the "open door policy." Parent's or staff don't have to schedule to meet with me, if my door is open, I'm available. This practice can take up some of your time, however, the value is immeasurable. Putting off parents or staff is not a reputation you want to be known for. With my policy, I know about the new stranger who moved in the neighborhood the morning the moving van pulls out of his driveway, while a principal who puts off parents and staff, finds out there is a paedophile in the neighborhood after their first victim is missing. You must create a culture of collaborative communication.

Know that if your hands haven't touched it, it will not get done. That is the nature of the educational profession. The Principal is the beginning and the end. You will have to get comfortable with this, even though it may take sometime to understand. Nothing happens without you. One reason for this, if it goes wrong, you ultimately will be the blame for it anyway. It's better to be proactive and at the forefront of everything that goes on in "Your" building.

One technique that I am consistently developing is the culture of debriefing sessions. You may notice this in the sports field, after a game, the coach and his staff will watch tape of the game to see what worked and what didn't work. Same here. Gather your key stakeholders after agenda items are completed and debrief. Discuss what's working, and what's not working. Remember you are the Captain of this ship. It's better to let a shipmate tell you there is a hole in the ship before it springs a leak, than to discover the leak after the ship has sank.

Lastly, a culture of collaborative communication will bring new ideas to your administration from outside of you. However, with the right environment, the authors of those ideas will want the credit to go to their leader who made it possible for their ideas to flow.

CULTURE OF COLLABORATIVE COMMUNICATION

CONFESSION- 10

"GREAT LEADERS ARE ALMOST ALWAYS GREAT SIMPLIFIERS, WHO CAN CUT THROUGH ARGUMENT, DEBATE, AND DOUBT TO OFFER A SOLUTION EVERYBODY CAN UNDERSTAND."
– GENERAL COLIN POWELL

IF YOU PASS IT, THEY WILL TOO.

CONFESSION- 11

A walk down the hallway with me might be a tad bit annoying. If I see something out of place, I don't wait to assign it to someone, I handle it as I'm aware of it. If it's paper on the floor, bulletin border falling or the cafeteria line wrapping out the door. If you pass, they will to.

CONFESSION- 11

My staff knows (or believes), I see it all and see more than I may acknowledge I'm aware of. These simple acts of not passing on an opportunity to fix the small things let's staff know you are aware of the larger things. This thwarts many of them on taking the calculated risk of believing you don't know what is happening at any given time. You have to make yourself present when your not. You know, how your mother was always present during your college days. You knew if you made that decision, mother would find out and the consequences would be severe. Likewise with the staff and students, they need to feel your presence, it keeps those minor task from becoming major problems.

Additionally, you have to show pride in your building and the importance of keeping the school clean and presentable. You also have to show that you are willing to step out of your role at times to take care of any task that presents itself. You don't have to schedule the custodians to pick up paper in front of you, you pick it up. However, you adjust the custodians schedule to visit this area of the building if the trash accumulation is increasing.

Do Not take this little act as insignificant, because many of our colleagues do. You are learning the proper way to lead a school and a staff. You are the first example and the standard bearer, so if you pass it, they will too.

IF YOU PASS IT, THEY WILL TOO.

CONFESSION- 11

"NOTHING SO CONCLUSIVELY PROVES A MAN'S ABILITY TO LEAD OTHERS AS WHAT HE DOES FROM DAY TO DAY TO LEAD HIMSELF."
- THOMAS J. WATSON SR.

THERE IS POWER IN NO

CONFESSION- 12

Of course you want to be a successful Principal, none of us take the job to become a failure. In this, you want your staff to be happy and productive. You treat them well and they feel respected. At the same time, you have to set the parameters that everything cannot be assumed as approved because of your kindness. Sometimes you have to say, "no". There is power in "No". **CONFESSION- 12**

This no is not with attitude or with malice, this no is to acknowledge that authority is present and is selective in enforcing. Not ruling with an iron fist, but making staff aware that there is a mental filter you process information or request through that may not always yield the response they favor.

The key to the no is not it's permanency, but its unpredictability. You have to keep all stakeholders on their toes as it relates to you. The no is unpredictable, but reliable. You are the standard bearer, the golden rule bearer, and the trendsetter of your building. You have the authority to move the crowd, start and stop the flow of the day, but you handle your authority with grace. There is a scripture in the Bible that states, " there was a hiding of his power." Use your authority wisely, but make sure you use it.

There was an instance in which a staff member rushed into my office with a perceived emergency. I immediately stopped what I was doing to hear what were the needs of this staff member. She began to explain to me how it was direly important that I let her run out of the building for only two hours and that she would return as soon as the emergency was resolved. I asked the staff member to share with me as much about the emergency as she could without going into her personal details.

As she began to explain what she needed to take care of, her requested time went down to an hour and a half, hour, then 30 minutes. The emergency changed to helping some one out of a situation. Needless to say, I told the employee, NO. We need you here and it sounds like your emergency can wait until you get off work.

This particular no was most effective due to the fact this particular staff member averaged 3 emergencies per month. (*Emergencies don't happen everyday*-PSM)

THERE IS POWER IN NO

CONFESSION- 12

"ANY ONE CAN HOLD THE HELM WHEN THE SEA IS CALM."
-PUBLILIUS SYRUS

ANSWER THE PHONE

CONFESSION- 13

Some days at school, the day will seem uncharacteristically smooth and uneventful. You are packing your bags and ready to set the building alarm for the evening. To your surprise, the phone begins to ring. It's true, often at this time of the evening, it's bill collectors because staff give the school number as their main number. But it doesn't matter, answer the phone. **CONFESSION-13**

On the other end of that call is often one of the 4 C's, Complaint, Concern, Conflict or Compliment.

Students have been home for an hour or two, but parents are just arriving from work to assess how their student's day transpired. That's when the phone begins to ring off the hook.

A story just doesn't sit well with the parent and they want someone to explain it better; immediately. If you are there to receive the desperate call, perfect. If you are not, depending on the severity, you'll end up on the other side of the phone call from the county office. If the parent is irate, they may call the school 30 times, if nobody answered or addressed their concerns, the next phone call will be the county/district office.

When parents make this call, the small situation gets a little more energy from either end and becomes an attention grabber. If the county doesn't answer or resolve it, you end up watching or hearing the story on the evening news from the investigative reporter who, answered the phone.

This unfortunate scenario can be avoided, by answering the phone. You have the ability to quail the situation by just being present. Listening to the parents concerns and offering your assistance in rectifying the issue on the following day.

This small habit will cause days to end smooth and mornings to begin without the line of parents out the door with previous days 4 C's, Complaints, Concerns, Conflicts, or Compliments.

Even though the last C does not happen much, one evening, I answered the phone late to my surprise. On the other end was a fifth grade mother. She first thanked me for answering the phone. She stated, " I just knew you were gone for the day or nobody would answer the phone." The mother then went on to thank me for creating the single gender classes. She shared that her twin daughters were going through anxiety about leaving elementary school soon, not being cool enough for boys and beginning to develop as young ladies. The simple change to having the single gender setting for their fifth grade year, allowed them time to go through these anxieties with other girls. This she attributed to me, Taking the risk. I received one of the rare C's that day, because I answered the phone.

" A GREAT LEADER'S COURAGE TO FULFILL HIS VISION COMES FROM PASSION, NOT POSITION."
-JOHN MAXWELL

BOOMERANG, I WANNA KNOW EVERYTHING

CONFESSION- 14

It's only fitting that, Boomerang, I want to know everything, follows Confession 13, "Answer the phone". Staff's have to make it a practice to tell you everything that has an impact on the students, staff members, parent, and the community. If the information is of a sensitive nature, you have to be made aware of it in a timely manner. Especially, since you are going to answer the phone in the evening. It makes a parent feel good when they call in despair and the Principal can say, " Teacher So and So, made me aware of the situation before they left for the day. I have this situation on my task list for the next morning." This shows the parent there is a culture of collaborative communication and the Principal has a pulse of what's going on in the building from the minor to major issues.

Without the information and the necessity to know everything, you will get blind sided often from parents, county office, issues in your building and appear very incompetent. When staff knows they need to make you aware of everything, they will head off trouble before it makes it to your desk and intervene on your behalf. This small confession empowers stakeholders because it's better to bring the Principal a solved issue instead of an unresolved issue. Besides, all boomerangs comeback. You are going to find out eventually, staff will want to let you know the boomerang is coming instead of it knocking you unconscious. **CONFESSION- 14**

One evening, I answered the phone and on the other end was a special education parent furious about a situation that happened that day. Her wheel chair bound student was not changed the entire day and was soaking wet from urinating on his self during school. Rightly so, she was furious and I was too, however, because I was familiar with the situation, I was able to calm the parent down and ensure her I would deal with the incident in the morning.

All school issues will come back to your desk, you have to put procedures in place to handle whatever comes your way. Follow the confessions and you will be prepared.

BOOMERANG, I WANNA KNOW EVERYTHING

CONFESSION- 14

"LEADERSHIP DOES NOT ALWAYS WEAR THE HARNESS OF COMPROMISE."
- WOODROW WILSON

THE BUCK STOPS HERE.

CONFESSION- 15

One summer, I had to enroll my children into my neighborhood elementary and middle schools. This was the first time they would enroll in schools outside of the district I worked in, so I wanted to make personal visits, to feel the spirit of the schools. Unconsciously, with it being the summer, I dressed casual, meaning no suit or tie.

School A, I entered the school to a not so warm reception from the front office staff. As I inquired about the registration procedures, I was brushed off, ignored by the secretary and had to wait until she answered about 6 phone calls before acknowledging my presence (Remember this is the summer, the building is empty).

Once it was finally my turn, the secretary could not answer any questions I asked. Consequently, I asked to speak with the Principal. The secretary said he was not available and his schedule was booked for the next two weeks (needless to say, I saw his car in the principal parking space, its the summer only four cars in the whole parking lot).

At the conclusion of not getting anything accomplished, I quietly left my Principal business card at the desk and asked could he give me a call when his schedule permits.

School B was almost the mirror of school A and almost as if they were reading from a script of bad customer service. Same ending routine, quietly leaving my business card as I walked out.

To my amazement, both principals even

though their schedules were booked for the next two weeks, left me voice mails on my Principal office phone before I could make it to my school that afternoon.

This is a culture we must immediately change. Customer service rather good or bad represents you and honesty will always stand the test of time. Don't let your staff misrepresent you in your absence intentionally or unintentionally. This is the biggest detractor to a great school or organization. If this aspect of your new job is broke, change it immediately. The buck stops here on this one. **Confession- 15**

Don't let this kind of apathy, disrespect or misrepresentation occur because it ultimately shapes the perception that parents and stakeholders have of you unknowingly.

Anytime parents are brushed off or mistreated, their response is that the school brushed them off or mistreated them. When they say the school, that equates to the principal. Now unbeknownst to you, you have brushed off or mistreated parents. This reputation will spill over into the community quickly and now you have to participate in the damage control.

Don't let this happen, take every effort to train, educate or eliminate your front office staff. They are your first line of defense and the face of the school. If they don't represent you well they will misrepresent you even better. The buck will ultimately stop with you, so take action immediately.

"INNOVATION DISTINGUISHES BETWEEN A LEADER AND A FOLLOWER."
- STEVE JOBS

@ THE FORK IN THE ROAD, TRAILBLAZERS GO STRAIGHT.

CONFESSION- 16

My first year, I was assigned a mentor, a retired principal. Her task was to guide me through some decisions without the fear of being evaluated. This was cool. I was to be able to lean on her even if it seemed like I needed to vent about my boss (even though I never did, don't fall for that one) and she was to keep it to herself.

One day, she was sharing some old school advice and instructed me to walk a little harder in the hallways. To my disdain, I questioned, " What do you mean walk harder?" She wanted my teachers and students to hear me coming down the hallways and to hop into shape from the sound of my footsteps. I honestly thought she was joking, but when she offered to demonstrate the technique, I knew we came from different schools of thought.

There are many theories of how to lead effectively, how to administrate with confidence, and how to rule with an iron fist. All of these theories have a place and/ or school where the method maybe most effective. However, you cannot add a template to your leadership style, because it will never be yours.

You don't have to fit a mold, be just like you predecessor or imitate some other principal so much you forget who you are. Remember, at the fork in the road, trailblazers go straight. **CONFESSION -16**

Don't try to fit into some others perception of you, lead from within. Don't do things a certain way, just because you were told that's how it has always been done. **Be Bold. Be Innovative. Be Fearless. Be Brave. Be Different. Be One of a Kind. Be You.**

Get guidance from those you trust, but be unique, an original is always better than a copy.

@THE FORK IN THE ROAD, TRAILBLAZERS GO STRAIGHT.

CONFESSION- 16

"THE LED MUST NOT BE COMPELLED; THEY MUST BE ABLE TO CHOOSE THEIR OWN LEADER."
- ALBERT EINSTEIN

SURROUND YOURSELF WITH EINSTEIN'S

CONFESSION- 17

Rest assured, you will not know everything as it relates to aspects of the job. You want to be aware, but you will not be the expert all the time. That's OK. What's not OK is not knowing something and faking like you do. It's not necessary. When you create the culture in your building of improvement and empowerment, your staff will cover your shortcomings with pride.

In my data room, I have something called a Fear Factor Wall. This wall is for staff to place on the wall areas that they are not as comfortable with. This is not used to embarrass or humiliate any staff member, it's just the opposite.

As a community or school family, we use the cover down technique. Whatever weaknesses a team member has is covered by the strengths of another team/ family member until that weakness is turned into a strength.

An effective leader creates an atmosphere where failure is not punitive, but a learning experience. Likewise as Principal, it's OK to not know everything at all times. When you don't know, you defer to your Einstein's you've placed around you. **CONFESSION- 17**

These Einstein's are staff members, whom you know specialize in areas you are not as strong in. These staff members may have been hired or identified to have strengths in areas you are not as confident in. It's OK for them to know this as well, they will take pride in making you look

GOOD! Remember when we talked about the bullies having needs that haven't been met. As a new leader, when you realize there are aspects, new initiatives or programs you are not proficient in, defer to one of your Einstein's to become the expert in that area.

This also can be done through committees and teams. Example, I wanted to beautify the campus with some flowers and greenery. My current knowledge in this area is the Two Dozen Roses for $20 dollar special I get for my wife. This was not going to fly in the front of the building.

I put the request out to my staff and found we had a Master Gardener on our staff. I immediately commisioned her as committee chair of the newly formed beautification project and the rest is history.

When you are an effective principal, your staff will desire to help you. They know that your success is their success. If they can aid your leadership with their skill set, they will. You have to be humble enough to let help, help. Give them a chance and you will be surprised that all you need to be successful is probably already in your building.

"NEARLY ALL MEN CAN STAND ADVERSITY, BUT IF YOU WANT TO TEST A MAN'S CHARACTER, GIVE HIM POWER."
- PRESIDENT ABRAHAM LINCOLN

YOU ARE NOT A HERO UNTIL YOU SAVE SOMETHING OR SOMEONE

CONFESSION- 18

Mid year through my first year, the district office developed a study to assess the size of the school system and to identify clusters of schools that could possibly be identified as needing school consolidation(closing).

In this process, each individual school had to complete attendance audits on all students. This directive came from the deputy superintendent and building registrars were responsible for going through every file in the building to ensure attendance accuracy.

My registrar was thorough and found multiple students who were not in our attendance area. The directive from up top said to immediately identify these students and give them one week to be withdrawn. The registrar immediately sent the letters of withdrawal to parents and the time-line began unbeknownst to me.

The next day, the phone calls began and parents were pleading their cases. The secretary was thorough and many lost out to the new rule.

In fielding the calls, one parent pleaded with me to investigate their address, they felt the findings were in error. The parents shared this with my registrar, but she stood firm with what she believed to be accurate.

I agreed with the parents to take one last look and push the issue for verification.

Upon further verification or clearing from the transportation department, it was determined that there were two streets with similar names. One street's address was in our zone and the other out of our zone. To the pleasure of the parents, their child was able to stay at our school.

This process upset my registrar because she believed my checking behind her acknowledged my disdain for her work ethics. This was not the case, sometime you have to take risk for one child to save many more. Remember, you are not a hero until you save something or someone.
CONFESSION- 18

YOU ARE NOT A HERO UNTIL YOU SAVE SOMETHING OR SOMEONE

CONFESSION- 18

"I SUPPOSE LEADERSHIP AT ONE TIME MEANT MUSCLES; BUT TODAY IT MEANS GETTING ALONG WITH PEOPLE."
- MOHANDAS GANDHI

USED TO BE'S DON'T MAKE ANY HONEY

CONFESSION- 19

This confession, I can't take credit for, I heard my Minister use it often in sermons. " Used to Be's don't make any Honey!" **CONFESSION- 19**

When you take over a school, you will be inundated with, " This is how we used to do it, this is how it should be done, this is how we like to do it." That may be the case, but at some point, you have to draw the line in the sand and let the staff know that the past is just that, past. I have given your way a try, and now its time to make changes. It is true that " change" is the only thing consistent. However, in some instances, change has to be calculated.

Take time to assess those areas in which you desire to change. Use surveys and casual conversations with stakeholders to gain valuable information prior to making the changes you desire. One tip I use, is letting others tell me how important the change (in their minds) is before I even acknowledge my plan of how to make changes.

There was a situation in which I knew I needed to change the location of car riders and the area where the buses loaded/unloaded. I knew this would be a touchy move because the school had this process in place for years.

To begin the change in their minds before I "made" the decision, I probed several key stakeholders with opened ended questions. Ms./ Mr. SO and SO, I noticed a little confusion in the car rider/ bus area. Tell me a little bit about that process. (DON'T SAY A WORD, JUST LISTEN).

What would you do to improve this process? (DON'T SAY A WORD, JUST LISTEN). That's a great idea, I'm going to think about that. Thanks for your input.

A couple things to notice. ALWAYS GO to key stakeholders, you know, the school staff reporter, the know it all, a potential adversary. Every building has one or three. Asking them their opinion or expertise, gives them a perceived voice in a key decision being made and creates unsolicited buy-in. Additionally, when you finally voice the decision "you made", your new cheerleader will feel empowered and will become the mediator for any dissension of this new great change.

Following the confessions throughout this book will make that transition easier, because you have won over their trust and attained buy-in. When you know its time, stand your ground, be smart and corral buy-in from the used to BE'S for change.

USED TO BE'S DON'T MAKE ANY HONEY

CONFESSION- 19

"A LEADER TAKES PEOPLE WHERE THEY WANT TO GO. A GREAT LEADER TAKES PEOPLE WHERE THEY DON'T NECESSARILY WANT TO GO, BUT OUGHT TO BE."
- ROSALYNN CARTER, FORMER FIRST LADY

SYSTEMS OUTLIVE PEOPLE

CONFESSION- 20

One thing I learned early in the Principalship was that the book I kept looking for to show me the way, did not exist. Being an avid reader and having that thirst for the right way, caused me to look for that magic article, documentary, or manuscript (thus, this is why you are reading this book now). As a scholar, I was confounded that I hadn't come across a, " how to" guide for dummies in the Principalship (don't worry, wrote that one too). More directly, within my own school system, I expected a training or manual that outlined the key factors all Principal's could lean on. Nope; Nothing.

In the business world, we would look for an S.O.P., Standard Operating Procedures. The guide you could pickup if you opened a McDonald's restaurant in Idaho or Illinois, some things are constants and can be duplicated. In education, we have been slow in establishing this process (I'm not talking about cookie cutter reform projects). If system's are in place, they will outlive the changes in the Principalship that are inevitable. Systems outlive people. **CONFESSIONS- 20**

During your year one or two, take time to begin formulating your S.O.P. for the building you are in charge. How is the phone answered? Where is the backup key to the cafeteria? What school do we go to in an evacuation? What day are lesson plans do? Some of these examples sound simplistic, but if it's not in place, then these questions go unanswered.

Now let me be clear, I'm not talking about the staff handbook in which staff members never look at after pre-planning. I'm discussing the system of educating children, that if your entire staff got sick, a replacement staff could come into the school and survive until your staff returns.

For example, the second day of school, my second year as Principal, my wife goes into labor with our third child. I had to leave work and stay gone for three weeks.

Despite my absence, my staff was able to cover down because the systems were in place and our collaborative communication kept everyone on the same page even in my absence. Take it from one who didn't believe that the school would survive in my absence, it did.

System outlive people, if you prepare staff in your presence, they can handle it in your absence.

SYSTEMS OUTLIVE PEOPLE

CONFESSION- 20

"I CANNOT GIVE YOU THE FORMULA FOR SUCCESS, BUT I CAN GIVE YOU THE FORMULA FOR FAILURE: WHICH IS: TRY TO PLEASE EVERYBODY."
HERBERT B. SWOPE

VOLLEYING WITH YOUR ADVERSARIES

CONFESSION- 21

If you follow all of the Confessions that have been shared throughout this book, you will have a successful career as a Principal and a leader. You will enjoy your job and change lives for the better. But know, you will never win over EVERYONE. This was something that didn't sit well with me.

I have always been a people person and can honestly say I don't know of any personal enemies. As a Principal, I expected the same, have everyone on my cheering squad; Wrong. Some people in their very nature are opposed to leadership regardless of how good or bad it is. As a rookie Principal I figured that wouldn't apply to me, I'm implementing the Confessions. Well it did.

However, I used it to my advantage. Remember this, when washing clothes, you must use a detergent to agitate the dirt and stains if not, you're just running water and not cleaning your clothes. It's necessary to have some adversaries on your staff to keep you on edge for maximum progress. So I decided to use my adversaries by volleying with them.

CONFESSION- 21

How? When decisions would present themselves that were tough, I would call in my chief adversary and discuss the situation with them. I would share my recommendation and give them the floor to tear into my ideas. They were like sharks that smelled blood and dived right in for the kill. Knowing this ahead of time, I never took offense to what they said, it was my intentions all along to get them to give me their point of view and use it for my benefit.

Don't be afraid to give them a voice. Often your adversaries have a lot to say, because no one is listening to them otherwise. When you give them the floor to communicate or spew their venom, you will quickly realize how they really didn't have much to say about nothing (That's Grandma Slang).

However, your adversaries sharing their different point of views gives you the other side of the lens you can't always see. Is the glass half full or half empty? Relax, let them voice their opinions(in a controlled environment), you can handle it through the confessions you have learned.

VOLLEYING WITH YOUR ADVERSARIES

CONFESSION- 21

"IF YOU THINK YOU ARE LEADING AND TURN AROUND TO SEE NO ONE IS FOLLOWING, THEN YOU ARE JUST TAKING A WALK."
- BENJAMIN HOOKS

BON VOYAGE TO YOUR ISLAND

CONFESSION- 22

There is a movie out where there's a guy who's on an island all by himself. He has to fend for himself and solve every obstacle he encounters on his own. Even though it gets tough, there is no one there to lean on, or get another's perspective. This had to be a lonely life.

The Principalship is similar in some aspects. Sometimes, you will have to handle some task all by yourself. Even the Einstein's you've hired, your adversaries you volley with and those whom you collaborate with can not aid you. In this role, you will receive information at the wrong times that will weigh on your energies and you can't share with anyone. From staff cuts; to an ill staff, to budget woes. It's like the song, " Me, Myself, and I."

You are unique and special. This role calls for some forms of isolation. You have to find an outlet away from your role to maintain your ability to lead from the island. If you enjoy reading, spending time with the family or playing golf (my favorite). Whatever outlet you can find, that doesn't involve the school, do it.

You have signed up to do a job that can consume your every waking hour and part of your dreams. I know you've waited some time to get the title and the responsibility, but know to last in this role, you have to know when to shut it down and enjoy your island. **CONFESSION- 22**

"THE BEST EXECUTIVE IS THE ONE WHO HAS SENSE ENOUGH TO PICK GOOD MEN TO DO WHAT HE WANTS DONE, AND SELF-RESTRAINT TO KEEP FROM MEDDLING WITH THEM WHILE THEY DO IT."
-THEODORE ROOSEVELT

POSTMASTER STAMPS IT ALL

CONFESSION- 23

Have you ever had to get that envelope in the mail by a certain date and the only way to prove the accuracy of the time mailed was to get the Postmasters stamp? Without that stamp, your envelope is not guaranteed to have been submitted by the date or approved.

You want to be the postmaster of your building. It is imperative that nothing goes out from your post(school building), to the general public, parents, or community without your stamp of approval. The postmaster stamps it all. **CONFESSION- 23**.

When information goes home to parents or the community, right or wrong, it becomes the school gospel. You have to always check for accuracy or approval because it ultimately reflects you.

This will require planning on your teachers and yourself. This requires your open door policy lend availability to time for approval of information.

A teacher once sent home bus route changes that she believed to be accurate. The changes were gathered from the school system's website and the teacher photocopied the new routes for the parents. Without bringing the routes to my office for approval, the route sheet was sent home to her class. Little did the teacher know, I received an email with the updated routes and the school system's website had not been updated yet.

Needless to say, that Monday morning, the teacher had no students present in her class that were bus riders, the old route sheet she sent home was 30 minutes off the new route schedule and they all missed the bus.

The parents were livid by the fact that they were given misinformation. Additionally, some student's parents left them at the stops enroute to their places of employment. We had to send staff members to the stops to pickup students. A real nightmare, that could have been avoided by following the confession that (you) approve information before it goes to your school community.

It is time consuming, however, it is in your best interest to approve everything.

POSTMASTER STAMPS IT ALL

CONFESSION- 23

"PAY NO MIND TO THOSE WHO TALK BEHIND YOUR BACK IT SIMPLY MEANS THAT YOU ARE TWO STEPS AHEAD."-PSM

THE CHOIR HARMONIZES, THE INDIVIDUAL SINGS A SOLO.

CONFESSION- 24

It's always a beautiful sound to hear a choir harmonizing to that beautiful song. When they are in tune, all of the voices sound as if they were one voice, a melodious miracle.

As principal, the choir is not often a melodic sound you want to hear. The choir in this instance represents the collection of like minded staff, parents, stakeholders, etc. that have unified to come against your school goals or agenda. They all have come together for one main purpose, to oppose you.

This could become your demise if not acted upon swiftly and with a plan. To win over the choir, offer the soloist a part. Take the time to meet with the choir members one at a time. While this may become time consuming, you will get a chance to hear directly from the individuals in a setting where there is no one around for the choir member to impress or gain strength from. The choir harmonizes, but the individual sings a solo. **CONFESSION- 24** Use this technique, and you will be able to diffuse issues quicker than if you go after the choir as a whole.

"IF YOU DON'T STAND SINCERE BY YOUR WORDS HOW SINCERE CAN THE PEOPLE BE? TAKE GREAT CARE OVER WORDS, TREASURE THEM."
-LAO-TZU

IMMA, IMMA, DO IT FIRST, THEN TALK ABOUT.

CONFESSION- 25

Some people honestly have a stuttering problem. You can take speech classes, intentionally speak slower or become a selective mute. One pattern of speech that Principals must not adopt is **Confession- 25**, The Imma, imma, disease. This disease is when a principal constantly talks about what they are going to do, but never follows through on their intentions. As a principal your word must be bond, meaning that it never fails.

If you're saying you are going to do; complete; participate; evaluate, etc. You must be found completing what you say with your mouth. Principals who constantly adhere to the Imma, Imma disease will quickly loose the confidence of the stakeholders they are charged to lead. Say what you mean and mean what you say.

Parents believe that you honestly and sincerely have their child's best interest at heart. However, if you develop this habit or disease, you will plaque your leadership and eventually destroy your reputation as an effective principal.

"I AM A MAN OF FIXED AND UNBENDING PRINCIPLES, THE FIRST OF WHICH IS TO BE FLEXIBLE AT ALL TIMES."
-EVERETT DIRKSEN

I APOLOGIZE

CONFESSION- 26

One of my former Principals during my AP days had a strategy that I didn't initially take to.

During one of our many conferences with parents, she would give the parents an opportunity to express their concerns and would not rebuttal, just shake her head and acknowledge the information being shared. Then the **CONFESSION- 26**, I Apologize.

The first couple of times I heard this admittance, I almost jumped out of my chair. Some of these situations she was apologizing for were clearly not the error of the school or particular staff. But repeatedly, she would say, I apologize.

As a principal who has adopted this Confession, now I understand.

You as the principal are not apologizing for the particular situation, what you are apologizing for is the fact that you are engaged in this dialogue with the parent because necessary communication between the staff, school and the parent didn't happen.

These two words, regardless of how heated the conference began, the confession would put the control back in the hands of the principal.

What you are saying to the parent is, I understand, I am in control of the situation that you have made me aware of, and I now will handle the situation.

Always remember, in this business, we are in constant service to the public. We must never be the aggressor or appear to be distant from the realities our stakeholders deal with daily.

As educators and professionals, oftentimes our stakeholders may feel we are over confident and arrogant. We must constantly fight back this persona and reassure our stakeholders through our example that we care. This begins from behind your desk, with you.

Use this Confession, it works miracles.

I APOLOGIZE

CONFESSION- 26

"NEVER TELL PEOPLE HOW TO DO THINGS. TELL THEM WHAT TO DO AND THEY WILL SURPRISE YOU WITH THEIR INGENUITY."
- GENERAL GEORGE S. PATTON

FINDING A MENTOR

CONFESSION- 27

Oftentimes, I would find myself not being one to follow others way of leading. This mind-set has allowed me to develop my own style of leading. However, I have studied many of the experts in the field of educational and business leadership. By default, I don't have a specific mentor that I can suggest to you. You may find a veteran or rookie administrator that you may observe and aid you in shaping your unique leadership style. For me it's a mixture that makes a one of a kind style of mine.

I highly recommend that you develop no other style but your own. Study this book and others I share in the reading list, but remember to stay unique. Read through my suggested booklist to follow some of the leaders I have studied.

During my first year, I asked my regional superintendent to share with me which principal in his region that he believed to be the best example of an effective principal. Once identified, I scheduled to spend a day with that principal.

The visit was full of insight and guidance. The principal shared many strategies and techniques they developed over the years. The principal also talked about some of the mistakes they made over the years. This little time together gave me other perspectives which additionally shaped my style.

Don't be afraid to learn from colleagues, fellow educators, and business leaders. Spend the money and attend conferences, join leadership organizations, and frequent the bookstore. Your mentor may not be an individual, but a process you adopt as a habit. Find a mentor. **CONFESSION-27**

FINDING A MENTOR

CONFESSION- 27

"THE PRICE OF GREATNESS IS RESPONSIBILITY."
-WINSTON CHURCHILL

IF IT DOESN'T EXIST, MAKE IT.

CONFESSION- 28

As the school year continues to provide you with necessary experiences, your expertise will slowly formulate. You will eventually be able to feel confident about your leadership style and your staff will reflect this new expertise. As you and your staff merge and marry styles, don't be afraid to begin to tailor your environment to fit the specific needs of your students. In doing so, you will often find out that one size does not fit all.

Reform models, expensive programs, etc., do not work in every school. When the reform model is determined not to be designed for your school and its not, don't be afraid that if it doesn't exist, make it. **CONFESSION- 28**

During one of my school terms, my school system purchased a program to improve the reading levels of our students. The program grouped the students based off a pre-assessment and that score determined their reading groups during the reading block daily. The program worked OK in our building, but our true need was not our reading levels, it was our math.

To create a better situation for our current students, we tailored our math daily practices similar to the reform model and grouped our students based off their math pre-assessment.

The awareness of the needs of our building and not being afraid to take the risk, "because the intent was meant for good", it allowed us to develop the schedule. End result, the students became the benefactors of our efforts.

Principals, you are the leader, don't be afraid to create what you need to be successful.

IF IT DOESN'T EXIST, MAKE IT.

CONFESSION- 28

"IT IS BETTER TO LEAD FROM BEHIND AND TO PUT OTHERS IN FRONT, ESPECIALLY WHEN YOU CELEBRATE VICTORY WHEN NICE THINGS OCCUR. YOU TAKE THE FRONT LINE WHEN THERE IS DANGER. THEN PEOPLE WILL APPRECIATE YOUR LEADERSHIP."
– NELSON MANDELA

RUN THROUGH THE TAPE

CONFESSION- 29

This job is not to the swift, but the one who endureth to the end.

You are now a 12 month employee, you have no time off and vacation is consumed with emails. You have to now learn how to pace yourself for consistency. Many leaders start off fast in this role and pull up half way through the year with injuries. You will learn that you sprint for 9 months during the academic year, but the race has another leg(the summer) you have to take time and effort to perform well in. In this role you have to run through the tape or the finish line. **CONFESSION -29**

One strategy I have used; planning the calendar for the entire year at the beginning of the year. This sounds simple, but many schools don't. Some principal's send out a monthly calendar's that's good, but take the time and plan the entire year.

Even though our clients only come to school for 9 months, their parents work for 12 months. You have some parents that will never make PTA or conference night because they have to give their jobs a two week notice to get off. With your monthly newsletter, you only share 4 weeks of information at a time and some of that information covers the previous month. You have some vendors that offer free pep rallies, assemblies, give-aways, but those dates are selected early by those principals who plan the entire year in advance.

You will have the opportunity to add

dates along the way, but some dates are consistent year to year. It easier to get to the finish line, when you can see it.

Additionally, our job is a very taxing position. Every issue in the building for 180+ days filters through you. This can be draining and weigh on you. If you don't spread the work around, the load will be so heavy, you won't be able to function. Use this confession in order to run through the tape with the same energy and drive you began the school year with.

RUN THROUGH THE TAPE

CONFESSION- 29

COURAGEOUS CONVERSATIONS

CONFESSION- 30

I would like to thank you for purchasing and reading this collection of principles that have shaped my leadership style, my confessions. This book is dedicated to those like you and I that sincerely want to be the best in the role we have been appointed to serve in. This Principalship is such a rewarding job, however, if you don't work to become the best, this same job can be detrimental. You have what it takes to lead the next generation of leaders and this is just a guide to encourage you to feel comfortable tapping into the inner voice you hear daily that guides your leadership.

The last confession is called courageous conversation. **CONFESSION- 30** Throughout the book, you read these words a few times, courageous conversation. In the other sections, those mentionings were in regards to conversations with others. The courageous conversations I'm sharing with you now are those conversations with your self.

Principals, be that leader that you would want to meet at your child's school. Be that leader that you would like your mom to visit. Be that principal that remembers your name when you see them in the grocery store. Be that principal that shows up at the little league games and graduations. Be that principal that you can look in the mirror and see a smile.

When you don't see that principal, I just mentioned above, have that courageous conversation with yourself; challenge yourself; analyze yourself; evaluate yourself; confess to yourself; and correct yourself.

You are the best! You are the brightest! You are the chosen!

Congratulations, you are ***The Principal.***

Confession :

1. An open declaration of something about one's self.

2. To give evidence of.

3. **A statement of one's principles.**

RECOMMENDED BOOK LIST

Strength and Leadership- Tom Rath

Leadership on the Line- Ronald Heifetz

The Heart of Change- John Kotter

Good to Great- Jim Collins

Qualities of Effective Principals- ASCD

Walk the Walk- Alan Deutschman

Transforming School Culture- Anthony Muhammad

The Five Dysfunctions of a Team- Patrick Lencioni

How the Mighty Fall- Jim Collins

A Sense of Urgency- John Kotter

Why Gender Matters- Leonard Sax

Crucial Conversations- Kerry Patterson, Joseph Grenny, Ron McMillan and Al Switzler

Talk It Out- Barbara Sanderson

Through the Cracks- Carolyn Sollman

Zapp in Education- William C. Byham

10 Traits of Highly Effective Principals- Elaine K. McEwan

More Practical Advice for Principals- Albert Snow

Fierce Conversations- Susan Scott

The Tao of Leadership- John Heider

Creating Better Schools- Louis MacKay, Elizabeth Ralson

How Full is your Bucket?- Tom Rath & Donald O. Clifton

Fish!- Stephen C. Lundin, Harry Paul, John Christensen

Motion Leadership- Michael Fullan

What's Worth Fighting For in the Principalship- Michael Fullen

Lead with Luv- Ken Blanchard and Colleen Barrett

Our Iceberg is Melting- John Kotter

Building Engaged Schools- Gary Gordon

Leaders, Strategies for Taking Charge- Warren Bennis and Burt Nanus

First Break All The Rules- Marcus Buckingham and Curt Coffman

The Heart of Coaching - Thomas Crane

Doing Work You Love - Cheryl Gilman

194 High Impact Letters for Busy Principals - Marilyn Grady

Leadership as Lunacy - Jacky Lumby and Fenwick English

Push Has Come to Shove - Steve Perry

Developing the Leader Within You - John C. Maxwell

Failure is Not an Option - Alan Blankstein

The Big Book of Team Motivating Games - Mary Scannell & Edward Scannell

From Good Schools to Great Schools - Susan Gray and William Streshly

ABOUT THE AUTHOR

Patrick S. Muhammad, was born and raised in East St. Louis, IL, in June of 1975 to Robert W. Smoot, Jr. and M. Catherine Smoot. Patrick's siblings, Deidra Denise Smoot- Green and Robyn Kaye Smoot (1999), all excelled in academics and athletics. The inner city entrepreneurial version of the "Cosby" family, their two parent home was a centerpiece of the block and a gathering place for the children.

The upbringing in E. St. Louis also known as "East Boogie" is where Patrick attributes his tenacity and wherewithal. In elementary school, Patrick made his mark on the city during a routine science project through a balloon release at Dunbar Elementary. His balloon, filled with a card only addressed with his first name and the school mailing address traveled from Tudor Avenue to Ontario, Canada, landing his story in the cities only newspaper, The East. St. Louis Monitor.

Excelling in sports, Patrick was an early standout baseball player at the historical Jackie Robinson Khoury League. His ability to cover the field as a speedy shortstop and switch-hitting bunting phenomena lead him all the way to Lincoln High School Varsity team. However, it was at Lincoln, that his talents as a ferocious point guard and smart floor general overshadowed his early sport success in baseball.

Under the tutelage of legendary coach Bennie Lewis, Patrick's basketball talents landed him a scholarship to Kentucky State University and a ticket out of East Boogie. This 1993 Homecoming King, Student Athlete of the Year, and Most Likely to Succeed kid from Vogel Place was stepping out with a city on his back and a focus on a new horizon.

Kentucky State University nestled in the little town of Frankfort became the ideal place for Patrick to tap into his inner spirit and actualize his budding potentials. He stood out early on campus through his Midwest speech and the respected notoriety of his upbringing in East Boogie. On the basketball court, it was the same. Five games into his freshman season, the senior point guard and the coach's feud led to the senior leaving the team in the middle of a game. Down the bench, Coach William Byrd Graham placed his trust in his little floor general, best known as, "Smooooooooot." From that night to his senior year, Patrick led the Thoroughbreds as the starting point guard. Finishing his basketball career as the assist leader and the William Exum Student of the year, number (4) left his mark on the KSU campus. However, it was off the court that Patrick was transforming as a man.

Sitting in Integrated Studies (IGS) class, a gifted wordsmith named Dr. Patricia Muhammad, confounded Patrick through her knowledge of history and world affairs. Her class caused Patrick to spend all his hours off the court burning the midnight oil studying and searching the libraries for the source of the information Dr. Patricia eloquently delivered. This quest and thirst for more knowledge led to the newly elected Alpha Phi Alpha, Inc. President to convince his fraternity brothers to hop on a bus and attend the historical (1995) Million Man March. It was on that day, October 16th, the lifelong athlete transformed into the lifelong scholar.

Upon graduation from Kentucky State University in May 1997, the East Boogie native, loaded up his truck at headed to Atlanta, GA to further his quest for knowledge. With only his sister Robyn for family in Atlanta, Patrick quickly made a name for himself on the speaking circuit. From churches, mosques, recreation centers, and schools, the floor general was controlling audiences not with his passing of the ball but his parsing of words.

In 1998, while in search of part time work, his career choice was cemented. An offering to teach school by Dr. Percy Mack placed him in a Decatur, GA school. The same tenacity he applied to the field, court and his studies, propelled him to quickly rise in the field of education. In the fall of 2001, with his Master's in Education Leadership from Georgia State University (GSU) behind him, Patrick began his administrative career as an Assistant Principal. In (2004) he completed his Educational Specialist in Educational leadership from GSU. Nine years later (2010) he moved into the Principalship.

Over the past fifteen years, Patrick has evolved into a noted educational leader, lecturer and scholar. As a lone proponent of single-gender classes in public schools, his students have excelled above the national averages. It is during this same time he honed his skills as a noted author and publisher.

Under his parent company, PSM Enterprises & Services, he has developed RATHSI Publishing, Your Faith Farms and a non-profit Reaching Back 4U Global Foundation. To date Patrick has written five books, Little Librarian Girl, Wear My Shoes Please, Mom Where's My Dad, Confessions of a Principal, and The Principal Farmer. Additionally, through his publishing company, RATHSI Publishing, LLC, over 200 authors are now in print.

Now as a highly sought after professional speaker, Patrick travels the country telling his story and sharing his vision. With East Boogie still on his back, he has dedicated his life to inspiring all that he can touch with his motto, "Remember, the only way to achieve success, is to reach back and take someone with you!"

Patrick is married to Ishtar Muhammad and the proud father of one daughter, Ishlah, and two sons, Ishijah and Ishstafah. They currently reside on their farm outside of Atlanta, GA.

www.ingramcontent.com/pod-product-compliance
Lightning Source LLC
Chambersburg PA
CBHW021004090426
42738CB00007B/642